Magnificent
SNACKS
COOKBOOK

Magnificent SNACKS COOKBOOK

Written & Edited by: Kathryn L. Ramsay
Production & Design: Eric Coffey
Photography: Clinton Ashton
Publisher: Gary W. Adams

Magnificent Cookbooks Publishing Inc.
30 Mural Street, Unit 5, Richmond Hill, Ontario, Canada L4B 1B5

Printed in Canada

FOREWORD

SNACKS – the mere mention of the word brings many different foods to mind. Perhaps you recall a childhood favorite spread on a cracker, or maybe its a superb new hot hors d'oeuvre sampled at a recent party. We feel that a snack is many different things: it's a between-meal treat, an afternoon hors d'oeuvre, an evening nibble and sometimes even a meal in itself. Included in this book you will find over sixty recipes we've developed that can truly be called *Magnificent* SNACKS.

There is nothing simpler than preparing a snack to please just about anyone's taste buds. All of our recipes contain ingredients easily found in most supermarkets and fresh food stores. No special utensils or equipment is required for preparation of any of the recipes found within this book. To further assist you, we have prefaced our book with "Cooking Hints" to give some general guidance on preparing a 'magnificent snack'.

The *Magnificent* SNACKS Cookbook will provide you with many new recipes that are sure to become regulars for brunches, sandwiches or main courses. But this cookbook is more than just a collection of wonderful recipes, it's also a source of ideas and techniques that will enable you to create some original snacks using your old favorite recipes. Our convenient 'Mix & Match Index' (page 126) makes it easy to use the recipes in many different ways by experimenting with our sauces, fillings, toppings, pastries and marinades. Whether it's doing something as simple as using your own filling recipe to modify the Salmon Baguette, or creating a new cheese mixture for the Bacon Cheese Fingers, you will find the variations on these recipes are virtually endless.

One of the greatest advantages of these recipes is the amount of free time they allow the cook. Time enough to enjoy the company of the guests as well as the completed snack. These recipes are all easy to partially prepare ahead and involve only a small amount of last minute preparation. In some cases they can be totally completed ahead of time and refrigerated or frozen until later when all can enjoy.

Prepare a *Magnificent* SNACK for your next get-together and just listen to how many people remark "You always serve *Magnificent* SNACKS!"

COOKING HINTS

Our *Magnificent* SNACKS recipes have been fully tested to ensure that you'll achieve the same great results as those displayed in each full-color photograph. To further assist you, we have included some helpful hints to keep in mind as you prepare each of our recipes.

- Always buy the freshest, best quality ingredients available. Your snack can only be as good as the ingredients you begin with.

- All of our recipes have been designed to be easily followed by both the experienced chef as well as the novice. Carefully follow the directions in each recipe and great results are assured.

- Because seasonings are a matter of very personal taste, you may find your family or friends prefer more or less of a particular spice or herb. If a change is necessary take the initiative and adjust the quantity slightly so the results will better suit your tastes.

- Cooking times will vary depending on the accuracy of your range or oven (in regard to temperature). During the last minutes of cooking, you should note not only the cooking time, but also the final appearance of the food as it appears in the accompanying photographs.

- There is no specialized equipment required to make a *magnificent snack.* A blender or food processor is very handy but almost never a requirement. A deep fat fryer is also convenient although a heavy pot filled with several inches of oil will also do the job. Heat the oil to 350°F – 375°F (180°C – 190°C) being careful not to let it burn.

- You will notice that many of our recipes have several different parts to them (dips, marinades etc.). We've compiled a handy 'Mix & Match' Index of these at the back of the book that you can use to create some new snacks of your own.

- Our full-color photographs are designed to give you ideas for both garnishing and serving your snacks. You can have great fun experimenting with serving pieces and accompaniments.

- Many of the snacks in this book can be frozen upon completion and prepared with a moments notice. When you see ingredients on special buy them and take a few minutes to prepare a snack for later.

Whether you are preparing your snacks ahead of time or just before serving, we know they'll all become *magnificent* favorites at your house.

INDEX

For additional copies of ''Magnificent Snacks'', a handy order form is
included on the last page of this book.

Frittata

Yield: 16 - 20 Slices

INGREDIENTS

Butter	2 tablespoons	30 ml
Chopped green onions	2 cups	500 ml
Eggs	8 large	8 large
18% cream	1/3 cup	75 ml
Grated parmesan cheese	1/2 cup	125 ml
Salt	1/2 teaspoon	2 ml
Pepper	dash	dash
Pitted black olives	4 oz.	100 g

- Preheat the oven to 350°F (180°C).
- Melt the butter in a large skillet.
- Have ready a 10" spring form pan or shallow round ovenproof dish. Using a brush lightly butter the pan with a bit of the melted butter.
- Sauté the green onions in the melted butter until they are wilted.
- In a large bowl beat the eggs, cream, cheese, salt and pepper together.
- Stir in the green onions.
- Pour the mixture into the prepared pan.
- Slice the black olives and sprinkle them over the egg mixture.
- Bake the frittata in the preheated oven for 18 to 20 minutes or until it is firm in the center. Place it under the broiler for 3 to 5 minutes to brown the top. Serve either hot from the oven or at room temperature.

HINT: Try other ingredients in place of the green onions and black olives. As with omelettes the variations are virtually endless.

Crocked Cheese

Yield: 2-1/2 cups (625 ml)

INGREDIENTS

Cottage cheese	1/4 cup	50 ml
Ricotta cheese	1/4 cup	50 ml
Grated cheddar cheese	2 cups	500 ml
Butter	1/2 cup	125 ml
Chopped green onions	1/2 cup	125 ml
Beer	2 tablespoons	30 ml
Dijon mustard	1 teaspoon	5 ml
Paprika	1 teaspoon	5 ml
Salt	1/4 teaspoon	1 ml
Poppy seeds	1-1/2 teaspoons	7 ml

Garnish
Poppy seeds

- Combine all ingredients with an electric mixer or food processor. Blend well.
- Turn the mixture into a crock or serving bowl. Sprinkle additional poppy seeds on top for garnish.
- Refrigerate until ready to serve. Serve with crackers or breadsticks.

HINT: Half a pound of cheddar cheese will yield 2 cups of grated cheese.

Cocktail Puffs

Yield: 7 Dozen

Puffs

Water	1 cup	250 ml
Butter	1/2 cup	125 ml
All purpose flour	1 cup	250 ml
Salt	1/2 teaspoon	2 ml
Eggs	4 large	4 large

Asparagus Filling

Frozen asparagus	20 oz.	566 g
Cream cheese	6 oz.	170 ml
Blue cheese	6 oz.	170 g
Mayonnaise	1 tablespoon	15 ml
Egg	1 large	1 large

- Preheat oven to 400°F (200°C). Lightly butter cookie sheets
- Bring water and butter to a boil in a medium saucepan.
- Mix the flour and salt together.
- Remove the saucepan from the heat and stir in the flour. Return the pan to low heat and cook until the mixture forms a ball which pulls away from the side of the pan · about 1 minute.
- Remove the pan from the heat. Stir in the eggs one at a time being sure that each egg is completely mixed before you add the next one.
- Place marble sized pieces of dough on the prepared cookie sheets. Bake for 20 minutes or until the puffs are golden and very light to pick up. Cool on racks.
- Thaw the asparagus and pat it dry to remove all moisture. Chop it coarsely.
- In a food processor, blender or electric mixer mix all filling ingredients until blended.
- When ready to serve cut the tops off the puffs and remove any uncooked dough. Fill with the asparagus filling & replace the tops.
- Heat in a 350°F (180°C) oven for 8 to 10 minutes.

HINT: These puffs freeze very well and are suited to a multitude of fillings.

Baked Camembert

Yield: 4 Servings

INGREDIENTS

Camembert	1 wheel	1 wheel
Brandy	1 teaspoon	5 ml
Sliced almonds	1 tablespoon	15 ml
French stick	1 loaf	1 loaf

- Several hours before serving take the camembert from the refrigerator and remove all wrapping. Using a toothpick pierce the skin of the cheese in several places. Pour the brandy over so that it sits on top of the cheese and can soak in.
- At serving time preheat the oven to 300°F (150°C).
- Arrange the almonds decoratively over the top of the cheese and place it in an ovenproof dish.
- Bake the cheese for 20 minutes. The almonds should be golden in color.
- Remove the cheese to a serving plate. Surround it with slices of bread.

HINT: This recipe is for a small wheel of camembert which is readily available in all grocery stores. If you are having a large party a cheese shop can provide you with a large wheel to serve 12 people or more. You must use a whole wheel of cheese. If you only use a slice the cheese does not have a rind all around to contain it as it melts.

Antipasto

Yield: 6.5 Quarts (6.5 L)

INGREDIENTS

Cauliflower	1 lg. head	1 lg. head
Green salad olives	24 oz.	750 ml
Pitted ripe olives	14 oz.	398 ml
Sweet pickled onions	24 oz.	750 ml
Celery	4 stalks	4 stalks
Zucchini	2 medium	2 medium
Green peppers	3 large	3 large
Sweet red peppers	3 large	3 large
Plum tomatoes	28 oz.	796 ml
Mushroom pieces and stems	30 oz.	852 ml
Flat anchovy fillets	4 oz.	112 g
Flaked tuna	13 oz.	368 g
Vegetable oil	1 cup	250 ml
Green beans	28 oz.	796 ml
Ketchup	32 oz.	946 ml
Hot ketchup	12 oz.	375 ml
White vinegar	1/2 cup	125 ml

- By hand, chop the cauliflower, olives, onions, celery, zucchini, peppers and tomatoes.
- Drain the liquid from the mushrooms, anchovies and tuna. Rinse the anchovies and tuna under hot water. Chop the anchovies and break up the tuna.
- Combine the vegetable oil, cauliflower, olives and onions in a large pot and cook over high heat for 10 minutes stirring frequently.
- Add all other ingredients except the anchovies, tuna and vinegar and cook an additional 10 minutes, stirring frequently.
- Add the achovies, tuna and vinegar and cook another 10 minutes, stirring frequently. Set aside to cool.
- Put the antipasto in sterilized jars and store in a cool place. It will keep for many weeks.

HINT: Make this with a friend as an afternoon project and split the finished product. This always makes a hit as a gift for friends.

Phyllo Triangles

Yield: Approximately 5 Dozen

INGREDIENTS

Frozen phyllo dough	1 pkg.	1 pkg.
Melted butter	1/2 cup	125 ml

Smoked Salmon Filling

Smoked salmon	4 oz.	100 g
Ricotta cheese	1 cup	250 ml
Egg yolk	1 large	1 large
Chopped capers	2 tablespoons	30 ml
Chopped onion	1/4 cup	50 ml
Chopped fresh dill	1 tablespoon	15 ml

- Follow the package instructions for thawing and handling the phyllo dough. Do not hasten this process as it will affect the dough.
- By hand chop the smoked salmon into coarse pieces.
- In a blender, electric mixer bowl or food processor mix the ricotta cheese and egg yolk together. Add all other filling ingredients and mix until blended. Don't overmix because you still want the salmon in small pieces.
- Remove one sheet of the phyllo dough and lightly butter it. Cover it with another sheet of dough and butter it again. Be sure to keep the unused phyllo well covered with a damp cloth.
- Cut the double-layer of phyllo crosswise into 5 strips and place a teaspoon of the filling at the end of each strip. Fold each strip by taking the bottom right corner over to meet the left side and making a triangle pocket. Fold the filled pocket over at its open edge. Repeat in alternating directions until you have reached the end of the strip. It's just like folding a flag.
- Butter the top of each triangle and place them on a greased cookie sheet. They may be either refrigerated or frozen for later use or baked immediately in a preheated 350°F (180°C) oven for 10 to 15 minutes or until golden and flaky. If the triangular pockets are frozen they need not be thawed before baking.

HINT: These can be frozen for several months in a sealed container and are ideal for unexpected company. Once you have mastered the technique there are numerous filling that can be used.

Cheesy Tortilla Chips

Yield: 60 Chips

INGREDIENTS

Tortilla or Nacho chips	60	60

Chili Cheese Topping

Grated cheddar cheese	1 cup	250 ml
Grated Monterey Jack cheese	1 cup	250 ml
Chopped red onion	1/3 cup	75 ml
Chopped red pepper	1/3 cup	75 ml
Black pepper	1/2 teaspoon	2 ml
Salt	1/4 teaspoon	1 ml
Chili powder	1/4 teaspoon	1 ml

- Preheat oven to 350°F (180°C).
- In a medium bowl combine the topping ingredients.
- Place 60 chips on an ungreased cookie sheet.
- Put 1 teaspoon of cheese on each chip. Bake for 5 to 7 minutes or until the cheese is melted. Serve hot.

HINT: The topping keeps well in the refrigerator. It's handy to have around for a quick snack. Try this topping on potato skins or crackers.

Won Tons

Yield: 7 Dozen

INGREDIENTS

Won ton skins	7 dozen	7 dozen
Oil for frying		

Wonton Filling

Uncooked shrimp	1/4 lb.	100 g
Ground pork	3/4 lb.	350 g
Chopped water chestnuts	1 cup	250 ml
Egg	1 large	1 large
Chopped green onion	2 tablespoons	30 ml
Soya sauce	1 tablespoon	15 ml
Dry sherry	1/2 teaspoon	2 ml
Minced ginger root	1 teaspoon	5 ml
Salt	1/2 teaspoon	2 ml
Minced garlic	1 clove	1 clove

Egg Wash

Egg	1 large	1 large
Water	1 tablespoon	15 ml

- Shell and devein the shrimp. Chop finely.
- Mix all the filling ingredients together and let the mixture stand
  for at least 30 minutes at room temperature or longer in the refrigerator.
- Make the egg wash by beating the egg together with the tablespoon
  of water.
- Place 1 teaspoon of filling on a won ton skin. Brush two adjacent
  edges of the skin with the egg wash. Fold the skin over and seal the
  moistened and unmoistened edges to each other to make a triangle. Brush
  one point of the long edge of the triangle with the egg wash and press
  it together with the other point. Refrigerate or freeze the won tons
  until ready to cook and serve.
- Heat the oil in a deep fryer according to appliance directions.
  Cook the won tons a few at a time for 3 to 5 minutes or until golden.
- Serve with soya sauce, plum sauce or our Oriental Dipping Sauce.
- **Oriental Dipping Sauce:** Dry Sherry - 1/3 cup (75 ml); Soya Sauce -
  1/4 cup (50 ml); Sugar - 1 teaspoon (5 ml); Chicken Broth - 10 oz. can
  (284 ml). Bring all ingredients to a boil in a small saucepan. Serve warm.

Stuffed Eggs

Yield: 2 dozen

INGREDIENTS

Eggs	12 large	12 large

Filling

Diced smoked turkey breast	1 cup	250 ml
Finely chopped celery	2 tablespoons	30 ml
Chopped seedless red grapes	1/3 cup	75 ml
Mayonnaise	2 tablespoons	30 ml
Chutney	1 teaspoon	5 ml

Topping

Mayonnaise	6 tablespoons	90 ml
Curry powder	1 teaspoon	5 ml
Salt	1/4 teaspoon	1 ml
Pepper	dash	dash

Garnish

Paprika

- Place the eggs in a large saucepan with enough salted cold water to cover them. Bring them to a boil, reduce the heat and simmer for 15 minutes. Run them under cold water immediately.
- Mix together the turkey, celery, grapes, mayonnaise and chutney. Stir well.
- Peel and carefully cut the eggs in half. Remove the egg yolks and place them in a bowl. Mix the yolks together with the mayonnaise, curry powder, salt and pepper until the mixture is completely smooth.
- Fill each egg white with the smoked turkey mixture until the filling is level with the top of the egg white.
- Put the yolk mixture in a pastry bag fitted with a large star-shaped tube. Pipe enough over each egg to cover the filling. Sprinkle each egg with paprika.
- Refrigerate until ready to serve.

HINT: Smoked turkey is now readily available in grocery stores and it imparts a special flavor to these eggs. If you prefer to use it, baked turkey is also delicious. These eggs are also great when stuffed with just the yolk topping.

Mushroom Turnovers

Yield: 5 Dozen

Cream Cheese Pastry

All-purpose flour	1-1/3 cup	325 ml
Butter	1/2 cup	125 ml
Cream cheese	8 oz.	225 g

Mushroom Filling

Butter	1/4 cup	50 ml
Finely chopped green onion	3 tablespoons	45 ml
Chopped mushrooms	8 oz.	225 g
Brandy	1 tablespoon	15 ml
All purpose flour	2 tablespoons	30 ml
Milk	1/2 cup	125 ml
Sour cream	1/2 cup	125 ml
Salt	1/2 teaspoon	2 ml
Black pepper	1/8 teaspoon	.5 ml
Cayenne pepper	1/8 teaspoon	.5 ml
Chopped parsley	1 tablespoon	15 ml
Chopped chives	1 tablespoon	15 ml
Lemon juice	1/2 teaspoon	2 ml

Place flour in a medium sized bowl. With pastry cutter blend in butter and then cream cheese. Form the dough into 2 balls and refrigerate them at least one hour before rolling. Melt butter in skillet. Add the green onions and stir until wilted. Add the mushrooms and brandy and cook 10 to 15 minutes over medium heat or until all the liquid is absorbed. Remove the skillet from the heat and stir in the flour and blend well. Add the milk and sour cream. Bring the mixture to a boil and cook for 1 to 2 minutes, stirring constantly. Remove the skillet from the heat and stir in the seasonings. Roll the pastry on a well-floured surface using a floured rolling pin. Cut circles 2½" in diameter. Place 1 teaspoon of filling on each pastry round and seal the pastry around it. Refrigerate or freeze until ready to use. Place the turnovers on a lightly greased cookie sheet. Prick the top of each turnover with a fork and bake in a preheated 350°F (180°C) oven for 15 minutes or until golden.

HINT: The pastry mixes beautifully in a food processor. You must freeze both the butter and cream cheese, cut them into pieces and add them gradually to the workbowl.

Greek Dip

Yield: 3 cups (750 ml)

INGREDIENTS

Frozen chopped spinach	10 oz.	283 g
Cucumbers	2 large	2 large
Feta cheese	4 oz.	100 g
Garlic	1 clove	1 clove
Plain yogurt	1 cup	250 ml
Chopped green onion	1/4 cup	50 ml
Pita bread	8 large	8 large

- Cook the spinach for 3 to 4 minutes. Drain and cool under cold water. Press all the water out of the spinach.
- Peel, seed and grate the cucumbers. Drain them of any water.
- Drain the feta and rinse it if it is packed in brine. Break it into very small pieces.
- Finely chop the garlic or put it through a garlic press.
- In a medium bowl stir the spinach, cucumber and cheese together with the chopped garlic, yogurt and green onion.
- Refrigerate the dip for several hours.
- Cut the pita bread into small wedges and place them on a cookie sheet. Toast them in a preheated 300°F (150°C) oven for 8 to 10 minutes. Allow to cool.
- Serve the dip surrounded by toasted pita bread.

Tarragon Chicken

Yield: 3 Dozen Pieces

INGREDIENTS

Chicken breasts	3 whole	3 whole

Tarragon Marinade

Oil	1 cup	250 ml
White wine	1/4 cup	50 ml
Fresh lemon juice	1/2 cup	125 ml
Chopped green onions	1/4 cup	50 ml
Dried tarragon	3 teaspoons	15 ml
Dijon mustard	2 teaspoons	10 ml
Salt	1/2 teaspoon	2 ml
Pepper	1/4 teaspoon	1 ml

Wooden Cocktail Skewers

- Bone the chicken breasts, split them and place them in one layer in a shallow dish.
- In a medium bowl combine all the marinade ingredients and pour the marinade over the chicken.
- Allow the chicken to marinate for 3 hours at room temperature or longer in the refrigerator. Turn the chicken once or twice while marinating.
- Drain the chicken and cut each breast into 6 strips. Thread each strip onto a wooden skewer.
- Brush each strip with a little of the marinade. The chicken can either be barbequed or broiled (placed approximately 6" below the preheated broiler) for about 5 minutes.
- Serve at once.

HINT: After the chicken has been threaded on the skewer you can wrap the rest of the skewer in foil to keep it from burning while the chicken cooks.

Eggplant Caviar

Yield: Approximately 3 cups (750 ml)

INGREDIENTS

Eggplant	1 large	1 large
Tomatoes	2 medium	2 medium
Chopped onion	1 medium	1 medium
Chopped garlic	2 cloves	2 cloves
Olive oil	3 tablespoons	45 ml
Lemon juice	1 tablespoon	15 ml
Salt	1/2 teaspoon	2 ml
Ground Savory	1/2 teaspoon	2 ml
Black pepper	1/8 teaspoon	.5 ml

Garnish
Parsley leaves

- To create the 'eggplant serving dish' place the eggplant on its side and determine which side will serve as the base. Cut off the top side in a shallow slice and hollow out the flesh leaving a 1/4"-1/2" shell. Rub the edge of the shell with lemon juice, wrap it tightly and refrigerate it.
- Chop the eggplant coarsely.
- Peel, seed and coarsely chop the tomatoes.
- Heat the olive oil in a large skillet and sauté the eggplant, tomatoes, onion and garlic for 5 to 6 minutes.
- Lower the heat, add the seasonings and simmer the mixture for 20 to 25 minutes.
- Remove the skillet from the heat and allow to cool to room temperature.
- In a blender or food processor coarsely chop the mixture. Chill it until serving time.
- When ready to serve fill the reserved eggplant shell and garnish with parsley.
- Serve with pita bread, party rye, breadsticks or crackers.

HINT: After cooking the mixture be sure to let it cool completely and chop it very briefly to retain the coarse appearance of the dip.

Crab Stuffed Mushrooms

Yield: Approximately 5 Dozen

INGREDIENTS

Mushroom caps	60 med.	60 med.
Juice of one lemon		

Crabmeat Filling

Chopped celery	1/2 cup	125 ml
Chopped onion	1/2 cup	125 ml
Creem cheese	1/2 cup	125 ml
Sour cream	1 tablespoon	15 ml
Breadcrumbs	2 tablespoons	30 ml
Lemon Juice	1 teaspoon	5 ml
Garlic powder	1/8 teaspoon	.5 ml
Salt	1/4 teaspoon	1 ml
Crabmeat	3/4 cup	175 ml

Topping
Paprika

- Wash the mushroom caps and break off the stems.
- Put the mushroom caps in a bowl with the lemon juice and cover them with boiling water. Let them stand one minute then drain them and pat them dry.
- In a blender, electric mixer bowl or food processor combine all the filling ingredients except the crabmeat and blend well.
- Stir the crabmeat into the mixture by hand and blend just until the crabmeat is incorporated.
- Fill each mushroom cap with the crabmeat filling and top it with a dash of paprika. Refrigerate them until serving time.
- Bake the mushroom caps on a lightly buttered cookie sheet in a 350°F (180°C) oven for 7 to 10 minutes.

HINT: Reserve the mushroom stems and use them in some of our recipes that use chopped mushrooms.

Marinated Shrimp

Yield: Approximately 40 Shrimp

INGREDIENTS

Medium shrimp	1 lb.	500 g

Marinade

Vinegar	1 cup	250 ml
White wine	1/3 cup	75 ml
Lemon juice	1 teaspoon	5 ml
Ground ginger	1/4 teaspoon	1 ml
Crumbled bay leaf	1 leaf	1 leaf
Whole pickling spice	1 tablespoon	15 ml
Salt	2 teaspoons	10 ml
Dijon mustard	1/2 teaspoon	2 ml
Vegetable oil	1/3 cup	75 ml
Chopped parsley	2 tablespoons	30 ml

- Bring 5 cups of lightly salted water to a boil. Add the shrimp and cook on high heat for 3 minutes. Drain the shrimp immediately and allow them to cool. Shell and devein them.
- In a medium saucepan combine the vinegar, wine, lemon juice, ginger, bay leaf, pickling spice, salt and Dijon mustard. Bring the mixture to a boil and cook for 5 minutes. Remove the pan from the heat and stir in the vegetable oil and parsley.
- Pour the marinade over the shrimp and allow the mixture to cool completely.
- Place the shrimp and liquid in a sterilized jar and store it in the refrigerator.
- At serving time remove the shrimp from the marinade and arrange them in a serving dish or bowl.

HINT: These keep very well in the refrigerator and can be made many days ahead of serving time.

Mini Pizzas

Yield: Approximately 7 dozen

INGREDIENTS

Flaky refrigerator biscuits	2 pkgs.	2 pkgs.

Tomato Sauce

Olive oil	1/4 cup	50 ml
Crushed garlic	2 cloves	2 cloves
Finely chopped onion	1/4 cup	50 ml
Finely chopped parsley	1/4 cup	50 ml
Tomato sauce	1 cup	250 ml
Plum tomatoes	2 cups	500 ml
Tomato paste	1 tablespoon	15 ml
White wine	1 tablespoon	15 ml
Dried basil	1 tablespoon	15 ml
Dried oregano	1 tablespoon	15 ml
Salt	1/4 teaspoon	1 ml
Pepper	dash	dash

Toppings

Anchovies, cooked ground beef, cooked italian sausage, hot peppers, mozzarella cheese, mushrooms, pepperoni.

- Heat the oil in a heavy skillet and sauté garlic, onion and parsley over medium heat for 5 minutes. Add all the other sauce ingredients and simmer 5 to 10 minutes.
- Butter a cookie sheet. Open the biscuits according to package directions. Each biscuit will have several layers of dough · separate the dough and use 2 or 3 pieces stacked together to make each mini pizza.
- Place the pizzas on the cookie sheet.
- Top each dough round with tomato sauce and the desired toppings.
- Bake the pizzas in a preheated 350°F (180°C) oven for about 10 minutes or until the crust is golden on the bottom. Serve hot.

HINT: You may bake the pizzas, freeze them and reheat them in a 350°F (180°C) oven for 3 to 5 minutes.

Honey Garlic Ribs

Yield: Approximately 2 Dozen Ribs

INGREDIENTS

Canadian back ribs	2 lbs.	1 kg
Paprika	2 teaspoons	10 ml
Garlic powder	1/4 teaspoon	1 ml
Water	4 teaspoons	20 ml
Liquid honey	4 tablespoons	60 ml
Chili sauce	6 tablespoons	90 ml

- Preheat the oven to 350°F (180°C).
- Cut the ribs into individual pieces.
- In a small bowl mix together the paprika, garlic powder and water and blend until it is thoroughly mixed.
- Rub each rib with the mixture using 3/4 of it, and place the ribs meaty side down in a baking dish. Bake them for 30 minutes.
- Turn the ribs and brush them with the remaining paprika mixture. Bake them for 10 more minutes.
- Mix together the honey and chili sauce and pour it over the ribs. Be sure to coat them evenly. Bake them another 5 to 10 minutes.
- Serve hot.

HINT: These can be done early in the day and reheated at time of serving by placing them briefly in a preheated 350°F (180°C) oven until they are warm. In place of ribs, try 2 lbs. (1 kg) of chicken wings · you'll get delicious honey garlic wings.

Sushi

Yield: 40 Slices

INGREDIENTS

Short-grained rice	2 cups	500 ml
Rice vinegar	1/2 cup	125 ml
Sugar	1/4 cup	50 ml
Salt	4 teaspoons	20 ml
Nori	5 sheets	5 sheets
Fresh ocean fish	8 oz.	250 g
Cucumber	1 medium	1 medium
Wasabi		
Soya sauce		

- Rinse the rice and cook it covered in 2 cups (500 ml) of boiling water over high heat for 5 to 6 minutes. Reduce the heat to medium for 5 to 6 minutes and then to low heat for 12 to 14 minutes. Remove from the heat and let it sit covered for 15 to 20 minutes.
- In a small saucepan cook the vinegar, sugar and salt over low heat until dissolved.
- Put the rice in a wooden or plastic bowl and pour 1/3 cup (75 ml) of the vinegar mixture over it. Stir constantly until the rice is cool.
- Toast the nori under the broiler until it turns bright green. This will take a minute or less.
- Place a sheet of toasted nori, shiny side down, on a towel and cover it with 1 cup of rice. Leave a 1" border at the top long edge.
- Cut the fish fillet and seeded peeled cucumber into 1/2" strips.
- Mix the wasabi according to package directions.
- Spread a little wasabi along the bottom edge of the rice. Place a line of fish fillet and cucumber over the wasabi. Roll up jelly roll fashion and press firmly to seal edges.
- Cut each roll into eight pieces and serve with wasabi and soy sauce on the side for dipping.

HINT: Wasabi (green horseradish), nori (dried seawood) and rice vinegar are all available in Oriental food stores. Sushi can be made several hours ahead if refrigerated. Remember to use only ocean fish such as tuna, snapper or ocean perch as fresh water fish should not be eaten raw.

Tuna Sponge Roll

Yield: Approximately 4 Dozen Slices

Sponge Roll

Butter	1/4 cup	50 ml
All purpose flour	4 tablespoons	60 ml
Hot milk	1-1/2 cups	375 ml
Salt	1/8 teaspoons	.5 ml
Sugar	2 teaspoons	10 ml
Chopped fresh dill	1 tablespoon	15 ml
Fresh nutmeg	pinch	pinch
Separated eggs	4 large	4 large
All purpose flour	6 tablespoons	75 ml

Tuna & Peppercorn Filling

Canned tunafish	13 oz.	368 g
Chopped green pepper	1/4 cup	50 ml
Crushed green peppercorns	1 tablespoon	15 ml
Mayonnaise	2 tablespoons	30 ml
Plain yogurt	1 tablespoon	15 ml
Lemon juice	1/2 teaspoon	2 ml
Salt	dash	dash

Line a sheet pan 17" X 11" X 3/4" deep with parchment paper and butter and flour the bottom and sides. In a large saucepan melt the butter and stir in 4 tablespoons of flour. When it is blended add the hot milk gradually and stir until thickened. Bring the mixture to a boil, turn it down and simmer for 3 to 4 minutes. Add the salt, sugar, dill and nutmeg. Beat the egg yolks lightly and stir into the sauce. Allow the sauce to cool to room temperature. Beat the egg whites until stiff but not dry. Fold one-third of the whites and 2 tablespoons of flour gently into the sauce. Repeat twice more until the ingredients are completely blended. Spread the batter onto the prepared pan. Bake in a preheated 400°F (200°C) oven for 5 minutes. Reduce the temperature to 300°F (150°C) and bake for 30 minutes. When baked turn it onto waxpaper and roll it crosswise immediately into a roll about 2" in diameter. Cool to room temperature. Mix all the filling ingredients together in a blender or food processor. When the roll is cool, unroll it, spread with filling, reroll and refrigerate until ready to slice and serve.

Piquant Seafood Dip

Yield: 2-1/2 cups (625 ml)

INGREDIENTS

Fresh or frozen perch	1 lb.	500 g
Butter	1 tablespoon	15 ml
Salt & pepper	to taste	to taste
Cream cheese	4 oz.	100 g
Sour cream	1/2 cup	125 ml
Chopped onion	1/4 cup	50 ml
Horseradish	2 tablespoons	30 ml
Capers	2 tablespoons	30 ml
Lemon juice	1 tablespoon	15 ml
Worcestershire sauce	1 teaspoon	5 ml
Salt	1 teaspoon	5 ml
Chopped pimento	3 tablespoons	45 ml

- Dot fish fillets with butter and sprinkle them with salt and pepper. Cook frozen fillets according to package directions. Fresh fillets can be cooked for 10 to 15 minutes in a preheated 375°F (190°C) oven until they are flaky. Cool, skin and flake the fillets.
- In a blender, electric mixer bowl or food processor blend together all ingredients except pimento.
- Drain the pimento, pat it dry and stir it into the dip. Refrigerate until serving time.
- At serving time place the dip in a hollowed out vegetable or in a serving dish. Surround it with accompaniments such as vegetables, crackers and breadsticks.

HINT: It's important to flake the fish by hand to remove any bones still in the fillets.

Tuna Melt

Yield: 6 Sandwiches

INGREDIENTS

Corn tortillas	6	6
Butter	2 tablespoons	30 ml
Chopped green onion	1/2 cup	125 ml
Chopped green pepper	1/2 cup	125 ml
Chopped garlic	1 clove	1 clove
Tuna	13 oz.	368 g
Tomato sauce	1/4 cup	50 ml
Hot banana peppers	2 teaspoons	10 ml
Chili powder	1 teaspoon	5 ml
Tobasco	4 dashes	4 dashes

Topping

Grated Monterey Jack cheese	1-1/2 cups	375 ml
Sliced green onions		

- Preheat oven to 350°F (180°C).
- Melt the butter in a small skillet. Sauté the onion, pepper and garlic until wilted. Do not brown them.
- Combine the onion, pepper, garlic, tuna, tomato sauce, banana peppers and seasonings in a medium bowl.
- Put one-sixth of the tuna mixture on each tortilla. Top each with 1/4 cup (50 ml) of grated cheese and decorate with olive slices.
- Bake for 10 minutes or until the cheese has melted and the tuna is hot. Serve at once.

HINT: Try this recipe using cooked chicken instead of tuna. It's delicious too.

Pickled Mushrooms

INGREDIENTS

Mushrooms	2 lbs.	1 kg
White vinegar	1 cup	250 ml
Water	1 cup	250 ml
Salt	1 teaspoon	5 ml
Coriander seed	1 teaspoon	5 ml
Mustard seed	1 teaspoon	5 ml
Dill seed	1 teaspoon	5 ml
Dried thyme	1 teaspoon	5 ml
Minced garlic	1 clove	1 clove

- Wash the mushrooms.
- Combine the mushrooms and the other ingredients in a large pot. Bring . the mixture to a boil and cook over medium heat for 20 minutes
- Cool slightly. Pour mushrooms and liquid into a large sterilized jar.
- Refrigerate at least one day before serving.

Stuffed Olives

INGREDIENTS

Colossal pitted olives	2 - 6 oz. cans	350 g
Semi-soft cheese with garlic & herbs	1 - 4 oz. package	100 g

- Drain the olives and cut a small slice off the bottom of each.
- Put the cheese in a pastry bag fitted with a small star-shaped tube.
- Pipe the cheese into each olive and stand it on its end.
- Refrigerate until serving time.

HINT: It's easy to keep these ingredients on hand for last minute snacks.

Spicy Wings

Yield: 2 Dozen Pieces

INGREDIENTS

Chicken wings	12 whole	12 whole
Flour	1 cup	250 ml
Salt	1/2 teaspoon	2 ml
Cayenne pepper	1 teaspoon	5 ml

Sauce

Butter	1/4 cup	50 ml
Chili sauce	1/4 cup	50 ml
Lemon juice	1 tablespoon	15 ml
Worcestershire sauce	1 teaspoon	5 ml
Tobasco	1 teaspoon	5 ml
Chili powder	1/2 teaspoon	2 ml

- Cut chicken wings into 3 pieces at joints. Discard the tips.
- Combine flour, salt and cayenne pepper in a medium bag. Toss the wings in the flour one-half at a time until they are completely lightly coated.
- Heat the oil in a deep fat fryer according to appliance instructions. Fry the wings for 10 minutes, turning them often. Keep them in a warm oven until all the wings are fried.
- Melt butter. Combine with the sauce ingredients in a large bowl.
- Remove wings from the oven and preheat the oven to 325°F (170°C). Toss the wings in the sauce until they are completely covered. Place them on a cookie sheet and bake them for 5 minutes or until hot. Serve them at once with the dipping sauce.

Blue Cheese Dipping Sauce

Sour cream	3/4 cup	175 ml
Blue cheese	4 oz.	100 g

Crumble the blue cheese and mix it with the sour cream.

HINT: You may fry the wings early in the day. Warm them in the preheated oven then toss with sauce and bake them 5 minutes. The coating sauce may be made spicier with the addition of more chili powder or red pepper flakes. Experiment and you can make everyone's wings 'to order'.

Spicy Shrimp Dip

Yield: 2-1/2 Cups (625 ml)

INGREDIENTS

Cream cheese	8 oz.	225 g
Mayonnaise	1/3 cup	75 ml
Seafood cocktail sauce	1/2 cup	50 ml
Lemon juice	1 tablespoon	15 ml
Chopped green onion	3 tablespoons	45 ml
Chopped parsley	1 tablespoon	15 ml
Tiny shrimp	4-1/4 oz.	120 g

- Combine all ingredients except shrimp in an electric mixer or food processor. Blend well.
- Stir the drained shrimp in by hand.
- Chill until ready to serve

Nippy Cheese Logs

Yield: 4 Logs

INGREDIENTS

Cream cheese	8 oz.	225 g
Grated cheddar cheese	2 cups	500 ml
Blue cheese	4 oz.	100 g

Topping
Paprika

- Combine all the ingredients in an electric mixer or food processor.
- Divide the cheese into four portions. Using wax paper, roll each portion into a log about 3" long and 1½" in diameter.
- Top with paprika and wrap tightly.
- Refrigerate or freeze until ready to use.

Cocktail Franks

Yield: 40 - 50 franks

INGREDIENTS

Sour cream	1 cup	250 ml
Chili sauce	3 tablespoons	45 ml
Horseradish	1/2 teaspoon	2 ml
Caraway seeds	1 tablespoon	15 ml
Salt	1/4 teaspoon	1 ml
Butter	1 tablespoon	15 ml
Vegetable oil	1 tablespoon	15 ml
Cocktail franks	2 lbs.	1 kg
Flour	1 teaspoon	5 ml

Garnish

Caraway seeds	1 tablespoon	15 ml

- In a small bowl combine the sour cream, chili sauce, horseradish, caraway seeds and salt.
- Heat the butter and oil in a skillet.
- Drain the franks of any liquid. Brown them in the skillet over medium high heat, stirring often, for about 5 minutes or until lightly browned.
- Remove the skillet from the heat. Remove the franks from the pan and keep them in a warm oven. Add the flour to the skillet and stir until it is mixed with the butter and oil. Return the pan to medium heat and cook, stirring constantly, for 1 minute.
- Add the sour cream mixture to the skillet and stir until the mixture has thickened.
- Place the franks in a chafing dish or preheated serving dish and pour the sauce over them. Sprinkle with caraway seeds.

HINT: Guests can serve themselves using cocktail forks or picks. If cocktail franks are unavailable use regular hot dogs cut into 1" pieces.

Mozzarella Mushrooms

Yield: 4 - 5 Dozen

INGREDIENTS

Medium mushrooms	1 lb.	500 g
Mozzarella cheese	4 oz.	100 g
All purpose flour	1/2 cup	125 ml
Eggs	2 large	2 large
Water	1 tablespoon	15 ml
Breadcrumbs	1 cup	250 ml
Oil for frying		

- Carefully remove the stems from the mushrooms and save them for another use. Wash and pat the mushroom caps dry. Cut the cheese into small cubes and put a cube inside each mushroom cap. Beat the eggs together with water.
- Roll each mushroom in flour, then the egg wash and finally the breadcrumbs. Be sure to cover the area where the mushroom and cheese join, and this will keep them together while they are cooking. Heat oil in the deep fat fryer according to appliance instructions.
- Cook mushrooms until they are a dark golden color. Drain them on paper towels and serve them hot with the dipping sauces.

Horseradish Dipping Sauce

Mayonnaise	1/2 cup	125 ml
Lemon juice	2 teaspoons	10 ml
Horseradish	2 teaspoons	10 ml
Dijon mustard	1 teaspoon	5 ml

Mix together. Chill until ready to use.

Cucumber Dipping Sauce

Sour cream	1/4 cup	50 ml
Mayonnaise	1/4 cup	50 ml
Chopped seeded cucumber	1/3 cup	75 ml
Fresh dill	1 tablespoon	15 ml
Pepper	dash	dash

Mix together. Chill until ready to serve.

Marinated Vegetables

Yield: A Large Bowl

Vegetables
Broccoli, carrots, cauliflower, celery, cherry tomatoes, green pepper, mushrooms, summer squash, sweet red pepper, zucchini.

Marinade

Vegetable oil	1/2 cup	125 ml
Olive oil	1/4 cup	50 ml
Red wine vinegar	2 cups	500 ml
Lemon juice	1 tablespoon	15 ml
Dry mustard	1 teaspoon	5 ml
Crushed garlic	2 cloves	2 cloves
Dried tarragon	1 teaspoon	10 ml
Sugar	2 tablespoons	30 ml
Salt	1/2 teaspoon	2 ml
Black pepper	1/8 teaspoon	.5 ml

- In a blender or large jar mix the marinade ingredients together.
- Wash all the vegetables and break or cut them into bite-size pieces. Place them in a large bowl.
- Pour the marinade over the prepared vegetables. Refrigerate the vegetables for at least 12 hours. While they are marinating toss them several times so they marinate evenly.
- At serving time drain the vegetables and arrange them in a large bowl or on a plate.

HINT: If you have any leftovers keep them refrigerated in a tightly sealed container. They will be delicious for snacks for several days.

Mexican Layered Dip

Serves approximately 15 people.

INGREDIENTS

Re-fried beans	1-16 oz. can	500 g
Ground beef	1/2 lb.	225 g
Hot pork sausage	1/2 lb	225 g
Chopped onion	1 medium	1 medium
Salt	1/2 teaspoon	2 ml
Chili powder	1/2 teaspoon	2 ml
Ground cumin	1/2 teaspoon	2 ml
Green chilies - drained	4 oz.	100 g
Grated Monterey Jack cheese	1 cup	250 ml
Medium or hot taco sauce	1 cup	250 ml
Finely chopped lettuce	1 cup	250 ml
Sour cream	3/4 cup	175 ml

Garnish

Chopped green onions	5 medium	5 medium
Pitted black olives - sliced	1/2 cup	125 ml
Stuffed green olives - sliced	1/2 cup	125 ml

- Put the beans in the bottom of a casserole dish at least 9" in diameter.
- Brown the beef, sausage and onions in a skillet. Season with salt, chili powder and cumin while cooking. Drain and cool slightly. Put it evenly over the beans.
- Chop the green chilies, reserving a few pieces for garnish and place the balance over the meat.
- Spread the grated cheese over the dish.
- Top with taco sauce.
- Refrigerate at least one hour to let the flavors blend. Up to this point the recipe can be made a day in advance.
- At serving time preheat the oven to 400°F (200°C) and bake the dip for 30 to 35 minutes.
- Top with lettuce and spoonfuls of sour cream. Arrange the garnish.
- Serve with corn chips, nacho chips or tortilla chips.

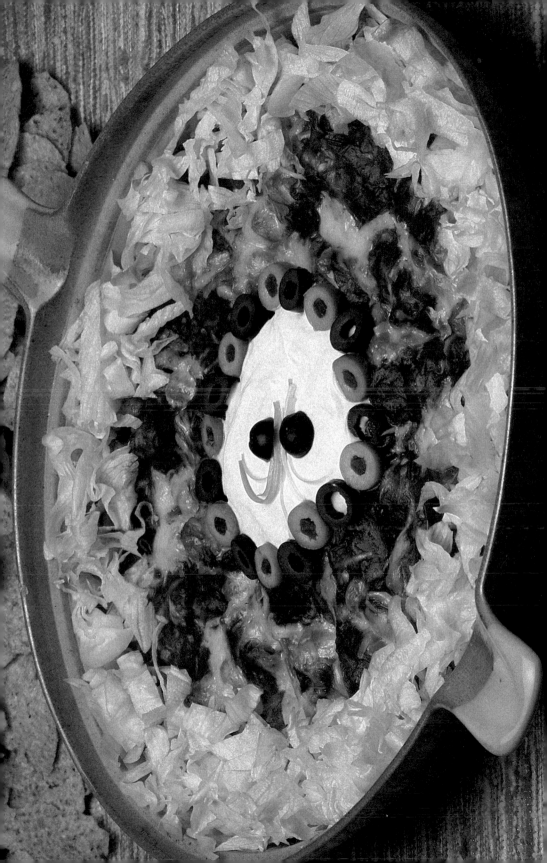

Bagna Cauda

Yield: 2 cups (500 ml)

INGREDIENTS

Butter	2 tablespoons	30 ml
Olive oil	2 tablespoons	30 ml
Garlic	3 cloves	3 cloves
Anchovy fillets	2 oz.	56 g
Flour	1 tablespoon	15 ml
Heavy cream	2 cups	500 ml

- Heat the butter and oil in a heavy skillet.
- Crush or very finely chop the garlic cloves. Sauté them in the butter and oil over medium heat for 3 to 5 minutes.
- Drain the anchovies well and chop them. Add them to the skillet and sauté them over medium heat for 2 minutes.
- Remove the skillet from the heat and add the flour. Stir until the mixture is smooth. Return it to medium heat and cook for one minute, stirring constantly.
- Add the cream to the mixture and stirring constantly, cook over medium high heat for 5-6 minutes or until the mixture is bubbling and thickened.
- Put the dip in a chafing dish, fondue pot or on a hot tray and serve warm with vegetable crudites or french bread.

HINT: It is very important to stir constantly while preparing this recipe. This unique dip should be served immediately after making because it is difficult to reheat.

Stuffed Grape Leaves

Yield: Approximately 60

INGREDIENTS

Bottled grape leaves	8 oz. jar	225 g
Pine nuts	1/4 cup	50 ml
Feta cheese	8 oz.	225 g
Uncooked orzo	1 cup	250 ml
Chopped parsley	1/4 cup	50 ml
Dried basil	1 teaspoon	5 ml
Salt	1/8 teaspoon	.5 ml
Pepper	1/8 teaspoon	.5 ml
Olive oil	1/2 cup	125 ml

- Drain the brine from the jar of grape leaves. Remove the leaves being careful not to break them. A long handle in the jar helps to compact them to get them out. Unroll the leaves, rinse them, clip any stems and lay them out flat on a work surface with the vein side up.
- Place the pine nuts on an ungreased cookie sheet and toast them for 5 minutes in a preheated 350°F (180°C) oven. Chop them coarsely.
- Drain the feta cheese and rinse it if it has been packed in brine. Break the feta into fine pieces.
- Combine the cheese with the nuts, orzo, parsley, basil, salt and pepper.
- Put 1 teaspoon (5 ml) of filling on the base of each leaf. Roll each leaf tightly enclosing the filling. Place each roll tightly against the others in an ovenproof dish.
- Combine the olive oil with enough water to completely cover the grape leaves. Pour the mixture over the leaves.
- Bake the stuffed leaves in a preheated 350°F (180°C) oven for 20 to 25 minutes.
- Cool the leaves to room temperature and refrigerate them in the cooking liquid. Serve them chilled and drained of cooking liquid

HINT: Orzo is a pasta that looks like rice. It is found in most grocery and bulk food stores in the pasta section.

Salmon Patties

Yield: 18 Patties

Patties

Eggs	2 large	2 large
Canned salmon	13 oz.	368 g
Dry breadcrumbs	1/2 cup	125 ml
Chopped onion	1/2 cup	125 ml
Chopped parsley	1/4 cup	50 ml
Lemon juice	1 tablespoon	15 ml
Salt	1/4 teaspoon	1 ml
Pepper	dash	dash
Dry breadcrumbs	3/4 cup	175 ml
Oil for frying	1 cup	250 ml

- In a medium bowl beat the eggs lightly with a fork.
- Add the other patty ingredients except the breadcrumbs. Stir until well mixed.
- Form the mixture into 18 small patties and coat each with the breadcrumbs.
- Cover the patties and refrigerate them at least 1/2 hour before cooking.
- Heat the oil in a shallow frying pan. Cook a few patties at a time, turning them once, until they are a deep golden brown on both sides. Drain on paper towels and serve hot with tartar sauce for dipping.

Tartar Sauce

Chopped capers	1 tablespoon	15 ml
Chopped green olives	1 tablespoon	15 ml
Chopped parsley	1 tablespoon	15 ml
Pickle relish	1 tablespoon	15 ml
Minced onion	1 tablespoon	15 ml
Mayonnaise	1 cup	250 ml

Mix well and refrigerate until serving time.

Chicken Pineapple Ball

Yield: 3-1/2 cups (875 ml)

INGREDIENTS

Cream cheese	8 oz.	225 g
Crushed pineapple	1/2 cup	125 ml
Cooked chicken	1 cup	250 ml
Chopped green onion	1/3 cup	75 ml
Chopped parsley	1/3 cup	75 ml
Chopped celery	1/3 cup	75 ml
Salt	1/4 teaspoon	1 ml
Pepper	1/8 teaspoon	.5 ml
Ground rosemary	1/4 teaspoon	1 ml
Walnut or pecan pieces	1-1/2 cups	375 ml

- Cream the cheese in a food processor or with an electric mixer.
- Drain the pineapple well.
- Break the chicken into small pieces.
- Add all the ingredients except the nuts to the cream cheese. Beat just until blended.
- Refrigerate the mixture for several hours.
- At serving time press the mixture into the desired shape and top it with the nuts. Serve with crackers.

HINT: One 6.5 oz. (184 g) can of cooked chicken will also yield enough for this recipe.

Fruit Dip

Yield: 1-1/2 cups (375 ml)

INGREDIENTS

Cream cheese	2 oz.	50 g
Ricotta cheese	1 cup	250 ml
Dark brown sugar	1 tablespoon	15 ml
Lemon juice	1/4 teaspoon	1 ml
Cinnamon	1/4 teaspoon	1 ml
Nutmeg	1/8 teaspoon	.5 ml

- Using an electric beater or food processor cream the cream cheese and ricotta cheese until light and fluffy.
- Add the other ingredients and beat again until smooth.
- Refrigerate until ready to serve.
- Serve with sliced apples, pears, peaches and other available fruits.

Herb Dip

Yield: 2 cups (500 ml)

INGREDIENTS

Cream cheese	4 oz.	100 g
Sour cream	6 tablespoons	90 ml
Chopped chive	1 tablespoon	15 ml
Chopped fresh thyme	2 tablespoons	30 ml
Chopped fresh watercress	1/4 cup	50 ml

- Mix all ingredients together.
- Refrigerate until serving time. Serve with vegetable crudites.

HINT: Experiment with the many fresh herbs now available and create your own tasty dips.

Cheese Surprises

Yield: Approximately 7 Dozen

INGREDIENTS

Grated cheddar	2 cups	500 ml
Butter	1/2 cup	125 ml
All purpose flour	1 cup	250 ml
Paprika	3/4 teaspooon	3 ml
Salt	1/2 teaspoon	2 ml
Medium stuffed olives	7 dozen	7 dozen

- With an electric mixer or food processor cream the cheese and butter together.
- Combine the flour, paprika and salt. Beat the flour mixture into the creamed mixture until the dough holds together.
- Drain the olives and pat them dry.
- Put one 1/2 teaspooon of the cheese mixture and an olive in your hands and roll them until the cheese completely covers the olive. Remember you want to put only enough cheese around the olive to form a thin crust.
- Put the covered olives on a cookie sheet and freeze them. When they are frozen store them in a tightly covered container or bag until ready to use.
- At serving time place the desired number on a cookie sheet and bake them at 450°F (230°C) for about 8 to 10 minutes. Serve at once.

HINT: These always make a hit at parties and because you can make them ahead they are a great item to have on hand.

Mini Quiches

Yield: 30 Tarts

Quiche Pastry

All-purpose flour	1-1/4 cup	300 ml
Salt	1/4 teaspoon	1 ml
Butter	1/2 cup	125 ml
Ice cold water	3 - 4 tablespoons	45 - 60 ml

Filling

Zucchini	2 medium	2 medium
Chopped onion	2 tablespoons	30 ml
Vegetable oil	1 tablespoon	15 ml
Dried oregano	1/8 teaspoon	.5 ml
Dried thyme	1/8 teaspoon	.5 ml
Dried marjoram	1/8 teaspoon	.5 ml
Eggs	2 large	2 large
18% cream	1 cup	250 ml
Dijon mustard	1/4 teaspoon	1 ml
Grated swiss cheese	1/2 cup	125 ml

- Make the pastry by stirring the flour and salt together. With a pastry blender cut in the butter until the flour resembles coarse meal. Add the water slowly just until the dough will form a ball. Divide the dough into 2 flattened balls and refrigerate them at least 1 hour.
- Preheat the oven to 400°F (200°C).
- Roll the dough and cut it into 2½" rounds. Place each pastry round in the ungreased cup of a mini muffin tin.
- Coarsely chop the zucchini. Sauté the zucchini and onion in the oil until tender. Stir in the oregano, thyme and marjoram.
- Beat the eggs, cream and mustard together.
- Put 1/2 teaspoon (2 ml) of the zucchini mixture in the bottom of each cup. Top it with a small amount of the grated cheese. Pour the egg-cream mixture over top.
- Bake for 5 minutes in the preheated oven. Reduce the heat to 300°F (150°C) and bake for 25 to 30 minutes. Cool the quiches for 10 minutes before serving.

HINT: The pastry can be made in the food processor but the butter MUST be cut in cubes, frozen and added gradually to the food processor. The dough can be put in the muffin cups early in the day and refrigerated, but make the filling at serving time.

Meatballs Burgundy

Yield: Approximately 6 Dozen

INGREDIENTS

Ground beef	1 lb.	500 g
Egg	1 large	1 large
Breadcrumbs	1/4 cup	50 ml
Finely chopped onion	1/2 cup	125 ml
Salt	1/2 teaspoon	2 ml
Pepper	1/4 teaspoon	1 ml
Dried thyme	1/4 teaspoon	1 ml

Burgundy Sauce

Butter	1/4 cup	50 ml
Garlic	1 clove	1 clove
All purpose flour	1/4 cup	50 ml
Beef bouillon	10 oz.	284 ml
Dry red wine	1 cup	250 ml

- Combine the ground beef, egg, breadcrumbs, onion, salt, pepper and thyme. Form into balls.
- Refrigerate the meatballs at least 1/2 hour.
- Melt the butter in a large skillet. Crush and sauté the garlic.
- Add the meatballs to the skillet and brown them on all sides. Remove them from the pan and keep them warm.
- Stir the flour into the juices remaining in the skillet. Cook, stirring constantly, for 1 minute.
- Add the bouillon and red wine. Cook until thick, stirring often.
- Place the meatballs in a serving dish and pour the sauce over them.

Zucchini Rounds

Yield: 3 Dozen Slices

INGREDIENTS

Zucchini	6 med.	6 med.

Gingered Pork Filling

Butter	1 tablespoon	15 ml
Chopped onion	2/3 cup	150 ml
Chopped garlic	2 cloves	2 cloves
Ground pork	3/4 lb.	350 g
Ground ginger	1/2 teaspoon	2 ml
Cayenne	1/2 teaspoon	2 ml
Tomato paste	1 tablespoon	15 ml
Dry white wine	1 tablespoon	15 ml
Salt	1/8 teaspoon	.5 ml
Pepper	dash	dash

- Wash the zucchini and cut them in 3" pieces. With a small sharp knife hollow out the center by removing all the seeds · be careful not to pierce the skin.
- Put the zucchini pieces in a pot of boiling water and cook them on high heat for 3 minutes. Drain them, run them under cold water and set them aside.
- In a large skillet melt the butter and sauté the onion and garlic until golden in color. Do not brown them.
- Add the meat and cook the mixture over high heat for about 10 minutes or until it is completely cooked. Drain on paper towels.
- Put the meat mixture in a blender or food processor and add all the other filling ingredients. Process until the mixture is finely ground.
- Carefully stuff the zucchini with the filling so they are firmly packed. Refrigerate them until ready to use.
- At serving time heat the stuffed pieces for 5 to 8 minutes in a 350°F (180°C) preheated oven. Slice them and serve immediately.

Salmon Baguette

Yield: Approximately 36 Slices

INGREDIENTS

Baguette or French Stick	1 loaf	1 loaf
Soft butter	2 tablespoons	30 ml

Salmon filling

Red salmon	6.5 oz	184 g
Finely chopped green pepper	1/3 cup	75 ml
Finely chopped green onion	1/3 cup	75 ml
Lemon juice	1/4 teaspoon	1 ml
Dried dillweed	1/2 teaspoon	2 ml
Mayonnaise	2 tablespoons	30 ml

- Cut the baguette into 6" lengths. Use a knife with a long blade to cut the center out of the bread leaving a 1/2" shell.
- Butter the inside of the baguette with the soft butter.
- Mix salmon, green pepper, green onion, lemon juice, dillweed and mayonnaise in a medium bowl.
- Spoon the salmon mixture into the hollowed out bread. Be sure to completely fill the shell with the filling. Wrap each piece tightly and refrigerate them until serving time.
- At serving time cut the baguettes into 1/2" slices. Garnish with relishes if desired.

HINT: Your family probably has lots of popular sandwich fillings that you could use with this technique.

Ham & Swiss

Yield: 2 cups (500 ml)

INGREDIENTS

Chopped ham	1 cup	250 ml
Grated swiss cheese	3/4 cup	175 ml
Cream cheese	2 oz.	50 g
Sour cream	1/3 cup	75 ml
Chopped green onion	2 tablespoons	30 ml
Coarse grained mustard	4 teaspoons	20 ml

Garnish
Chopped Dill Pickle
Fresh parsley

- In a medium bowl combine the ham, Swiss cheese, cream cheese, sour cream, green onion and mustard. Blend them together using a fork. Be sure to get the ingredients completely mixed.
- Refrigerate until serving time.
- At serving time mound the spread on a serving plate. Garnish with chopped dill pickle and parsley.
- Serve with cocktail rye bread or cut pieces of regular rye bread.

HINT: One 6-3/4 oz. can of ham can be used in this recipe. Just drain and shred it.

Skewered Beef

Yield: Approximately 24 Skewers

INGREDIENTS

Sirloin steak (3/4" thick)	1-1/2 lb.	750 g

Oriental Marinade

Sesame seeds	1/2 cup	125 ml
Salt	1/8 teaspoon	.5 ml
Green onion	1/4 cup	50 ml
Soy sauce	1/2 cup	125 ml
Vegetable oil	2 tablespoons	30 ml
Flour	1 tablespoon	15 ml
Sugar	2 teaspoons	10 ml
Pepper	1/8 teaspoon	.5 ml

Wooden cocktail skewers

- Preheat the oven to 350°F (180°C). Place the sesame seeds on a cookie sheet and bake them, stirring often, for 5 minutes or until they are golden.
- In a blender or food processor combine the toasted seeds and salt and blend until the seeds are pulverized. Add all the other marinade ingredients and blend until they are mixed.
- Cut the steak into strips about 4" long. Marinate them in the marinade for 15 minutes. Remove them from the marinade and rub off all excess marinade.
- Thread the beef onto cocktail skewers.
- The meat may be either broiled (place 6" under a preheated broiler) for about 5 to 7 minutes, or cooked to desired doneness on a barbeque.

HINT: The marinade can be made ahead and the beef cut into strips. Do not marinate the beef until you are ready to cook it. After you have put the meat on the skewer you can wrap the rest of the skewer in aluminum foil to keep it from burning while cooking.

Eggplant Rolls

Yield: Approximately 3 Dozen

INGREDIENTS

Eggplant	1 large	1 large
Salt		

Eggplant Filling

Salami	6 slices	6 slices
Grated mozzarella cheese	1 cup	250 ml
Grated parmesan cheese	3 tablespoons	45 ml
Egg	1 large	1 large
Dried basil	1/2 teaspoon	2 ml
Salt	1/8 teaspoon	.5 ml
Pepper	1/8 teaspoon	.5 ml
All purpose flour	1/2 cup	125 ml
Egg (lightly beaten)	1 large	1 large
Breadcrumbs	1 cup	250 ml

Oil for deep frying

- Peel the eggplant and cut it in very thin slices. Sprinkle each slice with salt and allow to sit for 1/2 hour.
- Wipe each slice to remove the salt and moisture.
- Chop the salami. Combine it with the mozzarella, parmesan, egg, basil, salt and pepper.
- Place a small amount of filling on each eggplant slice. Roll the slice and secure it with a toothpick.
- Roll the filled eggplant slice in the flour, then the egg and finally the breadcrumbs. Be sure the coating sticks to the folded area. Refrigerate the rolls at least 1 hour.
- In a deep fryer or a deep skillet heat the oil to 350°F (180°C). Fry the rolls a few at a time. When they are cooked drain them on paper towels, remove the toothpicks and serve them warm.

HINT: A large uniormly shaped eggplant gives you the most uniform slices for this finger food.

Stuffed Snow Peas

Yield: 6 Dozen

INGREDIENTS

Snow peas	6 dozen	6 dozen

Blue Cheese Filling

Cream cheese	4 oz.	100 g
Blue cheese	4 oz.	100 g
Sour cream	2 tablespoons	30 ml
Creamy horseradish	1 teaspoon	5 ml
Worcestershire sauce	1/2 teaspoon	2 ml
Tobasco	1 dash	1 dash

- Wash the snow peas. Steam them 1 minute over boiling water and rinse them immediately under cold water. Pat them dry.
- In a blender, electric mixer or food processor mix all the filling ingredients until creamy. Refrigerate 1/2 hour.
- Remove the stem from each pea pod and with a knife carefully slit open the center of the side to which the peas are not attached.
- Put the cheese mixture in a pastry bag fitted with a small star decorating tip.
- Pipe the cheese mixture into each pod and refrigerate them until ready to serve.

HINT: The snow peas are a refreshing accompaniment for cheese but this filling is equally good as a spread for crackers. When snow peas are available be inventive and try a few of the other fillings in this book. The cheese filling freezes well.

Diablo Dip

Serves approximately 10 people

INGREDIENTS

Avocados	2 medium	2 medium
Sour cream	1 tablespoon	15 ml
Lemon juice	1/2 teaspoon	2 ml
Salt	1/8 teaspoon	.5 ml
Pepper	1/8 teaspoon	.5 ml
Tobasco	3 dashes	3 dashes
Taco seasoning	2 tablespoons	30 ml
Grated brick cheese	1/2 cup	125 ml
Grated cheddar cheese	1/2 cup	125 ml
Finely chopped tomato	1 medium	1 medium
Finely chopped green onion	1/3 cup	75 ml
Sliced green & black olives	1/4 cup	50 ml

- Peel and mash the avocados.
- Mix together the avocados, sour cream, lemon juice, salt, pepper and tobasco. Mound the mixture in the center of a serving plate.
- Sprinkle the taco seasoning evenly over the avocado mixture.
- Layer the remaining ingredients over the avocado mixture. Refrigerate until serving time.
- Serve surrounded by nacho or tortilla chips or your favorite cracker.

HINT: The riper the avocados are the less sour cream you will need to add. Be sure to have the mixture thick enough so that it can be formed into a mound.

Chicken Paté

Yield: 2 cups of paté (500 ml)

INGREDIENTS

Belgian endive	5-6 heads	5-6 heads

Paté

Chicken livers	1 lb.	500 g
Butter	4 tablespoons	60 ml
Chopped onion	1 cup	250 ml
Chopped mushrooms	1-1/2 cups	375 ml
Dry white wine	1/4 cup	50 ml
Thyme	1/2 teaspoon	2 ml
Garlic powder	1/4 teaspoon	1 ml
Salt	1/4 teaspoon	1 ml
Pepper	1/8 teaspoon	.5 ml

Garnish

Chopped parsley	1/2 cup	125 ml

- Trim any fat from the chicken livers and pat them dry.
- Heat 2 tablespoons of the butter in a skillet. Sauté the onion until it is wilted but not browned.
- Add the remaining 2 tablespoons of butter. Add the chicken livers and mushrooms and cook the mixture on high heat for about 5 minutes turning the livers often to cook them completely.
- Remove the pan from the heat and add the wine and seasonings.
- Place the mixture in a blender or food processor and process until it is smooth. Refrigerate at least one hour.
- Break off the endive leaves, trim the ends and wash them and pat dry.
- Fit a pastry bag with a star tip and fill it with the paté. Pipe the paté onto the endive leaves. Dip each end in the chopped parsley for garnish. Arrange on a serving plate and refrigerate until serving time.

HINT: This paté is excellent with toast or crackers for less formal occasions. About 1/3 lb. of mushrooms will yield 1-1/2 cups of chopped mushrooms.

Cherry Tomatoes

Yield: 5 Dozen

INGREDIENTS

Cherry tomatoes	60	60

Artichoke Filling

Artichoke hearts	14 oz.	396 g
Grated parmesan cheese	1 cup	250 ml
Mayonnaise	1 cup	250 ml

- Cut a slice off the bottom of each washed tomato. Carefully remove the seeds and allow the tomato to drain upside down on paper towels.
- Drain the artichoke hearts. In a blender or food processor chop them finely.
- Add the cheese and mayonnaise to the artichokes and blend well.
- Fill each tomato using either a pastry bag fitted with a large tip or a very small spoon.
- Cover the tomatoes and refrigerate them until serving time.
- At serving time the filled tomatoes may be served at room temperature or heated for 5 minutes in a 375°F (190°C) preheated oven.

HINT: One quart of cherry tomatoes should yield about 60.

Escargots in Croustades

Yield: 24 Pieces

INGREDIENTS

Canned escargots	2 dozen	2 dozen
Butter	2 tablespoons	30 ml

Croustades

Unsliced white bread	1 loaf	1 loaf
Melted butter	2 tablespoons	30 ml

Pesto Sauce

Fresh basil leaves	1 cup	250 ml
Garlic	1 clove	1 clove
Pine nuts	2 tablespoons	30 ml
Grated parmesan cheese	1/4 cup	50 ml
Ricotta cheese	2 tablespoons	30 ml
Olive oil	1/4 cup	50 ml

- To prepare the croustades, cut the bread into 24 cubes about 1½" x 1" x 1". Carefully pull the center out to form a cup.
- Melt the butter and brush each bread cube with it. Toast the cubes in a preheated 400°F (200°C) oven for about 5 minutes or until golden. Set them aside until serving time.
- Prepare the pesto sauce by combining the basil leaves, garlic, pine nuts, parmesan cheese and ricotta cheese in a blender or food processor. Process until chopped and blended. With the machine running add the olive oil in a slow steady stream. Set aside until serving time.
- At serving time rinse the escargots and sauté them in a hot skillet with 2 tablespoons of butter.
- Place a dab of pesto sauce in each croustade. Top it with an escargot and some of the butter. Place another dab of pesto on the edge of each croustade.
- Place them under a preheated broiler for about 5 minutes or until the sauce begins to bubble.

HINT: Pesto sauce freezes well and is a versatile sauce that is excellent with hot and cold pasta as well as poultry. Make lots when fresh basil is available and enjoy it all year long.

Carrot Paté

Yield: 8 Slices

INGREDIENTS

Carrots	1 lb.	500 g
Butter	2 tablespoons	30 ml
Chicken stock	10 oz.	284 ml
Salt	1 teaspoon	5 ml
Pepper	1/8 teaspoon	.5 ml
Mushrooms	1/3 lb.	150 g
Minced green onion	1 tablespoon	15 ml
Vegetable oil	1 teaspoon	5 ml
Eggs	2 large	2 large
Grated swiss cheese	1/4 cup	50 ml
Chopped parsley	3 tablespoons	45 ml

Garnish
Fresh parsley

- Preheat oven to 425°F (220°C). Lightly butter the bottom and side of a 3 cup loaf pan or round mold. Line the bottom of the pan with buttered wax paper.
- Wash and peel the carrots. Slice them thinly.
- Melt the butter in a medium saucepan. Sauté the carrots for about 3 to 5 minutes.
- Add the chicken stock, salt and pepper and bring it to a boil. Boil covered for 5 minutes and uncovered for about 15 minutes. Drain off any chicken stock remaining. Chop the carrots finely.
- Chop the mushrooms finely. Sauté them with the green onions in the oil until tender.
- In a large bowl beat the eggs with a fork and add the carrots, mushrooms, cheese and parsley. Blend well.
- Place the mixture in the prepared pan and cover it tightly with foil. Place the pan in another pan of boiling water so that the water reaches 2/3 of the way up the sides of the filled pan.
- Bake for 30 to 35 minutes in the preheated oven. Refrigerate several hours before serving.
- At serving time carefully unmold the paté, remove the wax paper and garnish with additional parsley.

HINT: This is an elegant appetizer as well as a good side dish for light lunches.

Spicy Lamb Turnovers

Yield: 6 Dozen

Basic Pastry

All-purpose flour	2 cups	500 ml
Salt	1/2 teaspoon	2 ml
Butter	1 cup	250 ml
Water	6 - 7 tablespoons	90-105 ml

Spicy Lamb Filling

Ground lamb	3/4 lb.	350 g
Chopped pine nuts	1/4 cup	50 ml
Curry powder	1 teaspoon	5 ml
Ground coriander	1/4 teaspoon	1 ml
Salt	1/2 teaspoon	2 ml
Paprika	1/2 teaspoon	2 ml
Ice water	1/4 cup	50 ml
Olive oil	1 tablespoon	15 ml

Egg Wash

Egg	1 large	1 large
Water	1 teaspoon	5 ml

To make pastry combine flour and salt. Cut in the butter using a pastry cutter. Blend until the flour is the consistency of coarse meal. Add enough water to hold the dough together in a ball. Divide it in 3 pieces and refrigerate it at least one hour. Combine all the filling ingredients thoroughly but gently. Do not overmix or the filling will become pastelike. Refrigerate at least one hour. Roll out a piece of dough on a floured surface using a well-floured rolling pin. Cut the dough into 2½" circles. Stir together the egg and water to make the egg wash. Place a teaspoon of meat on the center of each circle. Brush the edge of each circle with the egg wash. Fold the pastry over the meat and press the edges together to seal them. Refrigerate or freeze until ready to use. Preheat oven to 350°F (180°C). Brush each turnover with the egg wash and pierce the top with a toothpick. Bake for 20 minutes or until golden.

HINT: The pastry can be made in the food processor but the butter must be frozen and added in small pieces. Pine nuts are available in bulk food and Italian groceries as well as many grocery stores.

Mushroom Croustades

Yield: Approximately 4 Dozen

Croustades

Thinly sliced white bread	2 loaves	2 loaves
Butter	2 tablespoons	30 ml

Filling

Mushrooms	1 lb.	500 g
Butter	1/4 cup	50 ml
Curry powder	2 teaspoons	10 ml
Ground coriander	1/4 teaspoon	1 ml
White wine	2 tablespoons	30 ml
Sour cream	1/3 cup	75 ml

Croustade Preparation
- Preheat oven to 400°F (200°C).
- Cut 2½" (6.5 cm) rounds out of each slice of bread.
- Butter mini muffin cups
- Fit a bread round in each muffin cup
- Bake at 400°F (200°C) for 10 minutes or until golden.
- Cool on racks.

Filling Preparation
- Wash,dry and chop mushrooms finely by hand or in a food processor.
- Melt the butter in a skillet. Sauté mushrooms for 2 minutes. Add curry powder, coriander and white wine. Cook the mixture over medium heat for 5 minutes or until all the liquid is absorbed.
- Remove the pan from the heat and stir in the sour cream.
- When ready to serve fill each croustade. Bake at 350°F (180°C) for 5 minutes or until heated.

HINT: The croustades can be made ahead and frozen for later use with a variety of fillings.

Apricot Halves

Yield: 18 Pieces

INGREDIENTS

Apricots	1 - 17 oz. can	483 g
Blue cheese	4 oz.	100 g
Toasted unblanched almonds	18	18

- Drain the apricots and pat them dry.
- Crumble the blue cheese. Press a small amount into each apricot half.
- Press a whole almond into the centre of the blue cheese.
- Refrigerate until serving time.

Tomato Cheese Wedges

Yield: 32 Pieces

INGREDIENTS

Tomatoes	4 large	4 large
Cream cheese	8 oz.	225 g
Pickapeppa Sauce	4 teaspoons	20 ml

- Wash each tomato and cut it into 8 pieces. Remove all seeds and membranes.
- Cream the cheese and Pickapeppa Sauce together.
- Fit a pastry tube with a star tip and fill it with the cheese mixture.
- Pipe some of the cheese onto each tomato slice. Refrigerate until serving time.

HINT: This is also a great cheese spread for crackers.

Touchdown Sandwich

Yield: 12 · 16 Slices

INGREDIENTS

Italian bread	1 loaf	1 loaf
Butter	2 tablespoons	30 ml
Sliced ham	1 lb.	500 g
Tomatoes	3 medium	3 medium
Mushrooms	1/3 lb.	150 g
Butter	1 tablespoon	15 ml

Cheese Sauce

Butter	3 tablespoons	45 ml
Flour	5 tablespoons	75 ml
Milk	1 cup	250 ml
Dry white wine	2 tablespoons	30 ml
Salt	1/2 teaspoon	2 ml
Cayenne pepper	dash	dash
Grated swiss cheese	3/4 cup	175 ml

Garnish
Paprika

Cut the bread in half lengthwise. Butter it with 2 tablespoons (30 ml of butter and toast it in a 350°F (180°C) oven for 10 minutes or until golden. Slice the tomatoes. Wash and slice the mushrooms and sauté them in 1 tablespoon (15 ml) of butter. Melt the 3 tablespoons (45 ml) of butter for the sauce in a medium saucepan. Remove it from the heat and stir in the flour. Return it to the heat and cook over medium heat, stirring constantly, for 2 minutes Add the milk and wine and cook stirring constantly until the mixture has thickened. Add the cheese and seasonings and stir until the cheese is melted. Layer the ham, tomato slices and mushrooms on the toasted bread reserving a few mushrooms for garnish. Top with the cheese sauce. Garnish with the remaining mushrooms and a sprinkle of paprika. Bake the sandwich loaf at 350°F (180°C) for 15 minutes. Serve at once.

HINT: If you prefer these can be made as individual sandwiches on split crusty rolls. The toasted bread and cheese sauce can be made ahead. Assembly should be done at serving time.

Salmon Tartar

Yield: 24 Pieces

INGREDIENTS

Fresh or frozen salmon	8 oz.	225 g
Olive oil	1-1/2 teaspoons	7 ml
Lemon juice	1 tablespoon	15 ml
Dried dillweed	1/2 teaspoon	2 ml
Chopped capers	2 teaspoons	10 ml
Chopped green onions	2 tablespoons	30 ml
Chopped parsley	1 teaspoon	5 ml
Butter	1 tablespoon	15 ml
Thinly sliced bread	6 slices	6 slices

Garnish

Black caviar	1 oz.	25 g

- Remove all bones and skin from the salmon. Chop it into very fine pieces. Do not use a blender or food processor or the fish will become pastelike.
- In a small mixing bowl combine the olive oil, lemon juice, dillweed, capers, green onion and parsley. Stir to mix.
- Fold the salmon into the mixture until it is well coated. Refrigerate the mixture several hours before serving.
- Melt the butter. Remove the crusts from the bread and brush each piece with some of the melted butter. Cut each piece into four triangles and place them on an ungreased cookie sheet in a preheated 425°F (220°C) oven for 8 to 10 minutes or until golden. Set aside to cool.
- At serving time put some of the salmon tartar on each toast point and garnish with the caviar.

HINT: This recipe may be doubled for larger parties. There are now varieties of inexpensive black caviar on the market and it makes this hors d'oeuvre truly special. A small whole caper can also be used for garnish.

Cheese Squares

Yield: 7 Dozen

INGREDIENTS

Butter	1/2 cup	125 ml
Chopped green onions	1/4 cup	50 ml
Butter	1 tablespoon	15 ml
Marinated artichoke hearts	12 oz.	340 ml
Eggs	10 large	10 large
All purpose flour	1/2 cup	125 ml
Baking powder	1 teaspoon	5 ml
Salt	1/8 teaspoon	.5 ml
Grated Monterey Jack cheese	1 lb.	500 g
Cottage cheese	1 pt.	454 ml
Chopped pimento	2 tablespoons	30 ml

- Preheat the oven to 400°F (200°C).
- Put the 1/2 cup of butter in a 13" x 9" baking pan and melt it in the oven while it preheats. Remove the pan as soon as the butter is melted.
- Sauté the green onions in the 1 tablespoon of butter.
- Drain and chop the artichoke hearts.
- In a large bowl beat eggs lightly.
- Mix flour, baking powder and salt together · add to eggs and beat lightly.
- Add the melted butter, chopped artichoke hearts, cheeses, pimento and green onions and mix to blend.
- Pour the mixture into the baking pan.
- Bake at 400°F (200°C) for 15 minutes then turn oven to 350°F (180°C) and bake for 40 minutes.
- Allow the squares to cool slightly before cutting and serving them.

HINT: These freeze beautifully after they have been cut. You can re-heat as many as you wish by putting them in a 350°F (180°C) oven for about 8 to 10 minutes.

Baked Shrimp

Yield: Approximately 40 Pieces

INGREDIENTS

Medium shrimp	1 lb.	500 g
Garlic	1 clove	1 clove
Hot pepper flakes	1/8 teaspoon	.5 ml
Lemon juice	2 tablespoons	30 ml

Garnish

Chopped parsley	2 tablespoons	30 ml

- Peel and devein the shrimp.
- Preheat the oven to 400°F (200°C).
- Chop the garlic finely or put it through a garlic press. Combine it with the hot pepper flakes and lemon juice.
- Toss the shrimp in the lemon juice mixture and arrange them decoratively in a single layer in a baking dish.
- Bake them in the preheated oven for 15 minutes.
- Garnish the shrimp with the chopped parsley. Serve warm.

HINT: A 9" round dish should hold the shrimp in one layer.

Baked Clams

Yield: One Dozen

INGREDIENTS

Butter	4 teaspoons	20 ml
All purpose flour	1 tablespoon	15 ml
10% cream	2/3 cup	150 ml
Salt	1/8 teaspoon	.5 ml
Pepper	1/8 teaspoon	.5 ml
Dijon mustard	1-1/2 teaspoon	7 ml
Parmesan cheese	1 tablespoon	15 ml
Butter	1 tablespoon	15 ml
Chopped onion	1 tablespoon	15 ml
Minced clams	6-1/2 oz.	184 g
Minced garlic clove	1 small	1 small
Chopped parsley	1 tablespoon	15 ml

Topping
Grated parmesan

- Melt the 4 teaspoons of butter in a small saucepan. Remove from the heat.
- Add the flour and stir it to blend. Return the pan to medium heat and cook the mixture for 3 minutes. Sir it constantly.
- Add the cream, salt and pepper and stir the mixture until it is thick. Simmer it over low heat for 15 minutes.
- Stir the mustard and cheese into the sauce. Cover it and set aside.
- In a small skillet melt the remaining butter and sauté the onion until it is softened.
- Add the clams and garlic and cook the mixture for 3 minutes.
- Add the clam mixture and the parsley to the sauce and stir.
- Spread the mixture evenly among 12 shells and sprinkle each with parmesan cheese. If you are making these early in the day cover and refrigerate them until serving time.
- Preheat the broiler and place the shells 6 inches from the heat for about 5 minutes or until they are golden and bubbly. Serve at once.

Oyster Fritters

Yield: 36 Fritters

INGREDIENTS

Canned oysters	16 oz.	500 g
All purpose flour	1 cup	250 ml
Salt	1/4 teaspoon	1 ml
Baking powder	1 teaspoon	5 ml
Egg	1 large	1 large
Sour cream	1 tablespoon	15 ml
Milk	1/2 cup	125 ml
Oyster juice	2 tablespoons	30 ml
Chopped parsley	1 tablespoon	15 ml

Oil for frying

- Preheat the oil in a deep fat fryer according to applicance directions.
- Drain the oysters reserving 2 tablespoons (30 ml) of the juice. Coarsely chop the oysters.
- In a large bowl mix the flour, salt and baking powder together.
- Beat the egg lightly with a fork. Stir in the sour cream.
- Make a well in the center of the flour mixture. Add the egg mixture, milk, and oyster juice. Stir just until all the ingredients are moistened. Fold in the oysters and parsley.
- Drop the batter carefully into the oil using two teaspoons. Cook the fritters for several minutes. They will be golden and firm to touch.
- Keep the cooked fritters warm in a 200°F (90°C) oven until all the fritters are cooked. Serve them at once with the dipping sauce.

Spicy Dipping Sauce

Mayonnaise	1/2 cup	125 ml
Worcestershire sauce	1 teaspoon	5 ml
Tobasco	1/4 teaspoon	1 ml

Mix the ingredients together. Cover the sauce and refrigerate it until serving time.

HINT: The dipping sauce can be made ahead but the fritter batter should not be mixed until serving time.

Potato Skins

Yield: 4 Pieces per Potato

INGREDIENTS
Baking potato

Cheddar Skins		
Grated cheddar cheese	1 tablespoon	15 ml
Chopped cooked bacon	2 teaspoons	10 ml

Mexican Skins		
Grated Monterey Jack cheese	1 tablespoon	15 ml
Jalapeno relish	2 teaspoons	10 ml
Sliced banana peppers	2-3 slices	2-3 slices

Garnish (optional)
Sour cream

These topping recipes are for one potato. You can make as many or as few of these delicious snacks as you wish.

- Preheat the oven to 350°F (180°C).
- Wash and dry each potato. Pierce with a fork and place in the preheated oven. Bake for 30 minutes or until the center is firm but can be easily pierced with a fork.
- Cool the potato, cut in quarters lengthwise and cut out the center leaving the skin with 1/4" to 1/2" of potato on it.
- Brush the skins with butter, sprinkle them with salt and pepper and arrange them on a buttered cookie sheet.
- Bake them at 350°F (180°C) for 10 minutes.
- Top them with either topping and bake for another 10 to 15 minutes or until cheese is melted and they are crispy.
- Serve at once.

HINT: If you wish you can bake the potatoes and make the topping earlier in the day, then assemble and proceed with final baking at serving time.

Bacon Cheese Fingers

Yield: 3 - 4 Dozen Pieces

INGREDIENTS

Butter	4 tablespoons	60 ml
Finely chopped green pepper	1/4 cup	50 ml
Finely chopped onion	1/2 cup	125 ml
Bacon Cheese Spread	10 oz.	284 g
Mayonnaise	2 tablespoons	30 ml
Seasoned salt	1/8 teaspoon	.5 ml
Garlic powder	1/8 teaspoon	.5 ml
Thinly sliced white bread	1 loaf	1 loaf

- Melt the butter in a small skillet. Sauté the pepper and onions over medium heat for about 5 minutes.
- In a medium bowl combine the cheese spread, mayonnaise, seasoned salt and garlic powder. Add the onions and peppers. Scrape the skillet well to remove all the butter. Blend all the ingredients well.
- Cut the crusts off the bread. Toast the bread in the oven or in a toaster until it is a light golden color.
- Spread the cheese mixture on the bread and stack two pieces together so you have bread, cheese, bread, cheese.
- Place the bread on a cookie sheet and freeze. Cut each piece into fingers or other desired shapes and keep them frozen until ready to use.
- At serving time bake them in a preheated 350°F (180°C) oven for 5 to 8 minutes.

HINT: If you cannot buy Bacon Cheese Spread use a processed cheese spread. Fry 3 strips of bacon until crisp, crumble them and combine them with the cheese spread for a delicious substitute ingredient.

Cheese Krispies

Yield: Approximately 9 Dozen

INGREDIENTS

Butter	3/4 cup	175 ml
Grated cheddar cheese	2 cups	500 ml
Cold pack sharp cheddar	1 cup	250 ml
Worcestershire sauce	1/2 teaspoon	2 ml
All purpose flour	2 cups	500 ml
Salt	1 teaspoon	5 ml
Rice Krispies	3 cups	750 ml

- Preheat the oven to 350°F (180°C). Lightly butter cookie sheets.
- In a large bowl cream the butter, cheeses and worcestershire sauce together using an electric mixer.
- In a medium bowl combine the flour, salt and Rice Krispies.
- Gradually add flour mixture to the cheeses and beat until the mixture is blended.
- Form the dough into small balls and place them on the prepared cookie sheets.
- Bake for 10 to 12 minutes or until they are firm to touch. Cool on racks.
- Store the Cheese Krispies in an airtight container or freezer until ready to use.

HINT: If you have not used your flour for some time sift it or put it through a strainer before measuring 2 cups. Do not use a food processor for this recipe as it will break up the Rice Krispies and affect the consistency of the baked Cheese Krispies.

Tuna Pita Pockets

Yield: 4 pieces

INGREDIENTS

Pita bread	2 large rounds	2 large
Butter	1 tablespoon	15 ml
Lettuce	4 leaves	4 leaves

Tuna Filling

Tunafish	6-1/2 oz.	184 g
Chopped green onion	1/4 cup	50 ml
Chopped celery	1/2 cup	125 ml
Seedless raisins	1/2 cup	125 ml
Chopped walnuts	1/3 cup	75 ml
Chopped seeded tomatoes	1/2 cup	125 ml
Mayonnaise	1/4 cup	50 ml
Sour cream	2 tablespoons	30 ml
Curry powder	1 teaspoon	5 ml
Salt	1/4 teaspoon	1 ml

Garnish

Bean sprouts	1/2 cup	125 ml

- Cut the pita in half and open the pockets. Butter each pocket. Line each with a lettuce leaf.
- In a medium bowl combine the tunafish, onion, celery, raisins, walnuts and tomatoes.
- In a smaller bowl combine the mayonnaise, sour cream, curry powder and salt. Pour it over the tuna mixture and blend.
- Fill each pocket with the tuna mixture. Garnish with bean sprouts.

HINT: If you wish, make the tuna filling ahead, but do not fill the pita pockets until serving time.

MIX & MATCH INDEX

ORDER FORM

For additional copies of this book, complete and mail this form to:

Magnificent Cookbooks Publishing Inc.

30 Mural Street, Unit 5, Richmond Hill, Ontario, Canada L4B 1B5

CANADA $11.95 + 1.00 (postage & handling) = $12.95
UNITED STATES $ 9.95 + 1.50 (postage & handling) = $11.45

Please send me_____copies of the "Magnificent Snacks" cookbook.
Please send me_____copies of the "Magnificent Cookies" cookbook.
Please send me_____copies of the "Magnificent Muffins" cookbook.

All cheques or money orders must be made payable to **'Magnificent Cookbooks'** and be submitted with this order.

Name . . . .

Address . . . .

City . . . .

Prov./State . . . . Postal/Zip . . . .

ORDER FORM

For additional copies of this book, complete and mail this form to:

Magnificent Cookbooks Publishing Inc.

30 Mural Street, Unit 5, Richmond Hill, Ontario, Canada L4B 1B5

CANADA $11.95 + 1.00 (postage & handling) = $12.95
UNITED STATES $ 9.95 + 1.50 (postage & handling) = $11.45

Please send me_____copies of the "Magnificent Snacks" cookbook.
Please send me_____copies of the "Magnificent Cookies" cookbook.
Please send me_____copies of the "Magnificent Muffins" cookbook.

All cheques or money orders must be made payable to **'Magnificent Cookbooks'** and be submitted with this order.

Name . . . .

Address . . . .

City . . . .

Prov./State . . . . Postal/Zip . . . .